Rescue Lines

Rescue Lines

by

Lesley Curwen

First published 2024 by The Hedgehog Poetry Press,

5 Coppack House, Churchill Avenue, Clevedon. BS21 6QW

www.hedgehogpress.co.uk

ISBN: 978-1-916830-33-2

For Mary

Contents

To a lifeboatman 9

Tricky fastenings 10

Sister with bees 11

irresistible pull 12

The allotment 13

Full sister half-known 14

Green-fingered 15

Recovery attempt 16

A view of Plymouth Breakwater 17

Afterness 18

How we witness the endurance of mothers and sisters 19

A novice learns to navigate 20

Thalassitude 22

What a sailing boat is 23

Dolphins sense grief on the water 24

The seas between us grow every day 25

SW Gale Force 8 expected midnight to 0600 26

Son et Lumiere 27

without end 28

unmoored 29

My sister's eye is opal 30

TO A LIFEBOATMAN

yellow arm stretched out to grip
  nerveless hands, we've got you mate

    coming in three two one, flung in like
      grey-skinned fish, slapped on deck

        in a heap, head crowned with salt, lungs
          blown like bellows, eyes blurred wet

          this is how we long to be saved

TRICKY FASTENINGS

Fifteen to do up, ecru silk, handsewn
slippery as ice, easy to fumble given
the limousine is idling in the road.

Worn fingers, nails painted (for once)
tenderly push buttons in tiny loops.
A sisterly service, one by one by one.

Both of us are leaking sweat and Arpege.
The fifteenth goes in. I sweep around
for your last skirt-tweak, shoulder-brush.

Out on the landing, we pause and fan.
Four hands find each other: your hot
grip says better luck than I ever had.

SISTER WITH BEES

She did not ask the bees to come. Their white noise
shudders skull and flesh. They cover her
damp nakedness.

She is passive, aware there is heart-stop pain behind
each furred thorax, starry compound eye. Her sweat is
honey. She is dressed to kill,

stands perfectly still beneath the hum, muscles cramped.
Barbed feet are rain on her white skin. A scarf of bees
ripples at her heart.

She does not move. Though her legs ache to run,
she has become used to holding herself in,
to their inevitable roar.

She is lulled by the intimacy of threat, speechless
at being chosen. She is sewn
in a venomed sheath.

After 'Girl with a Bee Dress' by Maggie Taylor

IRRESISTIBLE PULL

his first touch makes you gasp rattles your pulse as the urge to retreat hits the cortex like cocaine but you strike out of your depth craving connection more visceral where burning cold can be endured in faith that endorphins douse sharp pain and this bright belief repeats like an earworm over and over again though hands and arms are numb in his grasp and sea tangle slaps your wafted body whose eyes clog and sluggish blood ebbs to the still-hot core of you deserting feeble legs that can barely kick his shins but you summon a scrap of strength to beat for shore knowing as you always did that it would end like this

THE ALLOTMENT

Time-lapse would show your skittering
course between thyme and cosmos
feeding honesty and thrift, your
　　　　hardy perennials.

You raise seedlings, blunt fingers
lifting leaves with the deft touch
you used to change nappies
whip cream, pull up socks
　　　　hide your face.

In the warm outside, you are under
surveillance. Soft chimes herald texts
asking the same old questions.
Alone. At the allotment.
　　　　No. No. No. Yes.

FULL SISTER HALF-KNOWN

Machine stutters. Hands guiding the burden of cloth down lines of stitch,
we peer through our specs at the seam.
>   Your knuckles are thick just like mine.

We are like and not like. Same awkward noses, same troublesome feet.
You were unplanned, handed to strangers.
>   I was legitimate, winner-take-all.

Autumn rain steams the window. We lean in, suck pins, shoulders
touching, heads together like the infants
>   we once were who never met.

You followed our mother's pattern, fell for a man who threaded himself
into your days, embroidered his name
>   on your heart and sewed your mouth shut.

On the face of it, you appeared smooth enough. When I finally turned you over
to look, you were a Frankenstein wreck
>   of stabbed-in needles and raggedy knots.

We unravelled the tangle together. You tore out his bloodied name
with an unpicker. Now we hold up our finished skirt
>   in matching hands and hope for a neat reverse.

GREEN-FINGERED

In a glass corridor patients and staff tramp
purposefully past glowing garden borders.

Six times, we take this route on each chemo day.
I sense your primal urge to plant, prune, weed.

Good days, we walk outside. You name trees and shrubs,
we hatch allotment plans for the spring of next year.

When summer comes, I wheel you out, trying
not to bump your tender bones on jagged paths.

Today, we are quiet. A sparrow hops to your slipper,
looks at you in the chair. Breathless, you face each other.

RECOVERY ATTEMPT

Wave after wave broke
on your cropped head and
I grabbed
your swollen hand
aching to pull you
into an orange boat
where rescue breaths
would bring you back from
the edge
but our hands
got caught
on the rail of
the hospital bed.

A VIEW OF PLYMOUTH BREAKWATER

Some mornings it drowns in spring tide,
its heft of Dartmoor rock subsumed.

Other days, whiteness flies on grey in
plumed smash, high as this house

where I suck breath through storm and lull,
reading your words on the water's face

finding anger, my endless rage
in the pummelling of waves on stone.

AFTERNESS

the first night is the longest   when the universe
hangs larger   and emptier than before
        when the loved one's skin   is shedding its warmth
             to a cold sheet   when atoms of their breath

have not yet left the room   when their skin's dust
still sits on shelves   when floors have not been
        swept clean   when sea has departed the land
           and dawn is day one   in the afterness

HOW WE WITNESS THE ENDURANCE OF MOTHERS AND SISTERS

the unblinking surveillance   the ban on visitors
the stealing of passwords   the constant texting
the inevitable name pulsing in phonelight
the suffocation of what is scrawled
in birthday cards as
love

and when they are dead will nothing touch our pain
when the sins against them loom
like planets on a horizon
swallowing any light
we used to
share

what remedy is there to stop the contagion
from these our silent condemned
whose time of co-erced service
compressed their selves
like geisha-feet into
something tiny and
mangled

A NOVICE LEARNS TO NAVIGATE

She launched blind to wind and tide. Charts unmarked in lockers below,
she knew only to stick to the coast that pitched high through April rain.
She could not say circumnavigate without throwing up. Was solo

but not alone. With each helm-tweak she sensed something lost moving
at the wake, mast-high or fathom-deep. Grounded on rocks awash despite
cardinal-flash, somehow she floated off on a spring tide, was smacked

by southerlies up the Irish Sea, running free with shearwater, puffin,
harbour porpoise, Nato submarine. Each cliff she passed, dark or pale,
glowed with significance. Each steep wall held the same imagined face.

On she tacked through spill and roll to runic-haze of Western Isles, white-ruffed
extremis of John O'Groats and round the top to battleship-grey North Sea
past dead ports, live gas fields, turbine wings, vampire haunts,

past low marsh, treacherous shallows, cracked sea-walls that may not hold,
closed windows of second homes. Ears pinned for the minor-key dirge
of Spitway BellBuoy, eyes peeled for giant China ships inbound

to a Thames unload, then bluebirds, white cliffs, abandoned ribs
littered with wet buoyancy aids to the costa investment-banker where
thousands of masts do skeleton-dance down desirable rivieras.

Close-hauled, she saw Land's End whose long Atlantic swell
filled her ears and made her hurl and still an absence flew behind
the boat as dolphins scissored its bow, each leap a living smile.

She gybed to go north, through eight-knot tides spun faster
than a scared woman can run, past landslips, missing teeth
of ex-cliffs to Mersey's mouth, the freight it once consumed

a curse upon its docks and out of the shadows to the Isle of Man
a biscuit-toss away. Full circle she came, after a hundred days
though destination lost its meaning. There was nowhere left to sail.

Grief clung to her bow like a foul breeze. She had endured the worst
the world could throw, and it was time. Taking a cardboard
tube to the leeward side, she laid its ashes in sea's embrace.

THALASSITUDE

wavelets / chins tipped / hold sun's embrace
squirrel grey in livid rays/ their ranks of open lips
mouth sweetness/ at the eye of dusk
no swimmers here/ to rip their harlequin silk
to shreds/ of light

ashore/ sole-prints are shadowed/ by day's ebbing
gold/ swallowed in crosshatched expanse
of tide/ whose basketwork
convexities/ suck land's mauve loom
below/ a flight of cumulus

WHAT A SAILING BOAT IS

surf-flirter   storm-rover   passion-rider
gale-heeler wheel-roller diamond-eater
moon-craver whole-maker dolphin-lover
land-leaver crew-shielder   mile-hoarder
spray-drencher gull-racer   planet-cruiser
blue-bounder   anchor-rocker star-spotter
salt-cruster dream-stealer   prayer-holder
wander-luster   wound-healer soul-porter

DOLPHINS SENSE GRIEF ON THE WATER

Unbearably
you breathe while she does
not.

Eye-blest, breath-hopped
at apex of your leap I
spy glitters of why to
carry on.

Fly hard and high my friend
rise your jet body to light
teach me the old desire to
soar.

THE SEAS BETWEEN US GROW EVERY DAY

the first few weeks I watch
you fade beyond my horizon

        I lose your face in the sun

now in the compass-star
           dead centre
of a long sail at snail's pace
I glance aft
and know I have covered
a thousand miles of
      wetness
    boredom
danger

the heading
is immaterial
what matters is
the space
between   us

SW GALE FORCE 8 EXPECTED MIDNIGHT TO 0600

The whitest sails vanish at night. Yachts
are scudding ghosts whose crew see lights

spring up at every compass point, burning
with significance. We guess their source:

giant trawler, coaster, cardinal buoys,
lighthouse five miles off, ship metal-close.

Worse yet is imperceptible threat of rogue
containers, nomadic storm-scourged trees.

In hard southwesterlies hours elongate,
our rods and cones straining to apprehend

first greying, night-layers undone, slow
bleach of edge as blink-flash becomes boat

or quay. Things are reduced to dimensions
known. We see the hazards narrowly missed.

SON ET LUMIERE

crescent moon   sails free of cirrus cloud
        in the bay   carpet of flicker   fallen xmas trees
port buoy   *red* every two seconds
        starboard buoy   *green* every five
            & the danger-danger-danger *white* of cardinals
endlessly warning   stay east   or run aground

the bright eye of a yacht   tracks away from land
        red shines high at the pier   where war-planes waited
for a tow to fly   from the bone-cold Sound
        behold this glittered map   these water-roads
for trawler   submarine   row-boat   destroyer

across the earth   lights flash   a planet *winks* back

WITHOUT END

you were sitting with your back to me
and I asked you are you really gone for ever
a pause and you said   kindly but firmly   yes
and I said I don't know how to put this but
I am trying to believe we will meet again
is that right

and the sound went   though the picture stayed
and there was only an empty room with a chair
which was not your house but also was
and I wondered where you and billions more
hide in the creases of the universe

do you crowd in a drop of sea water
or mass in empty fields behind the milky way
waiting for the rest of us

UNMOORED

                              legs drift horizonwards
                        arms starfishwide palmsup
                  tendons & joints unhinge
          bodyparts recede
knots loosed
        I float un
                tethered
                      a skin of salt
                              healing
                                    bitterest sores

anger sea-urchin sharp
        reduced to ash
                deleted by the breeze
                        lines   slipped

MY SISTER'S EYE IS OPAL

set in gold. She stares up
from my right hand, a blue oval
creased and dappled red
whose conflagration is a memorial
of who she was, of how she lived
in dense cloud and bolts of
unexpected light. Of the propensity
to shine, to deliver a tiny neon
shock in crowding dark. Of mercy
shown by she who was starved of mercy,
of a lightning strike of grace
across a closed valley, of what
she left me, a mirror flashed
at each hand's turn, a face
that semaphores the urgent now,
the always pulse of the sun.

ACKNOWLEDGEMENTS

'To a lifeboatman' published in 'Breathless' by Snakeskin Poetry

'SW Gale Force 8 expected midnight to 0600' published in 'Tempest' by Green Ink Poetry